Breaking the Back of Generational Curses

A Journey to Wholeness Workbook

Doneita Harmon

Knowledge Power Books

ISBN: 978-1-7322665-1-3

Library of Congress Control Number: 2017954174

Edited by: Angela Witt
Cover Design: Juan Roberts, Creative Lunacy, Inc.
Literary Director: Sandra L. Slayton

Logo designed by: Danielle Nicole Harmon

Scriptures marked NAS are taken from the NEW AMERICAN STANDARD (NAS): Scripture taken from the NEW AMERICAN STANDARD BIBLE®, copyright© 1960, 1962, 1963, 1968, 1971, 1972, 1973, 1975, 1977, 1995 by The Lockman Foundation. Used by permission.

Scriptures marked TM are taken from the THE MESSAGE:
THE BIBLE IN CONTEMPORARY ENGLISH (TM): Scripture taken from THE MESSAGE: THE BIBLE IN CONTEMPORARY ENGLISH, copyright©1993, 1994, 1995, 1996, 2000, 2001, 2002. Used by permission of NavPress Publishing Group

Printed in the United States of America

Published by:
Knowledge Power Books
A Division of Knowledge Power Communications, Inc.
Valencia, CA 91355
www.knowledgepowerbooks.com

Table of Contents

Introduction 1

PART I: Assessment

Section 1: Identifying the Problem 5

PART II: Diagnosis

Section 1: Identifying the Solution 11

Section 2: The Origin of Generational Curses 12

Section 3: God as Judge 14

Section 4: Sin's Penalty 18

Section 5: How Does Generational Deliverance Work? 23

Section 6: Generational Deliverance, Why Now? 28

Section 7: The Purpose and Characteristics of Curses 31

PART III: Implementation

Section 1: Implementing the Solution 37

Section 2: Performing the Generational Deliverance Technique 40

PART IV: Evaluation

Section 1: Evaluating the Solution 43

Appendix A: Developing a Prayer Focus Using the
Generational Deliverance Technique 45

Appendix B: Generational Deliverance Prayer Strategy Guideline 47

Appendix C: Generational Deliverance Prayer Focus for Family Leaders 49

Appendix D: Generational Deliverance Prayer 51

Appendix E: Deuteronomy 28:1-68 (NASB) 53

About the Author 58

Breaking the Back of Generational Curses

A Journey to Wholeness

Workbook

Introduction

Welcome to my armory. Here is the room that contains my spiritual weaponry and is the place where Holy Spirit and I work together to determine the strategy that is to be utilized when performing Generational Warfare.™ Here is also the place where we will learn how to employ the strategy of Generational Deliverance™. This workbook was created to be used in concert with the book, *Breaking the Back of Generational Curses: Journey to Wholeness*. It will take you step by step through the generational deliverance process as introduced in the book. This work book will assist in helping you understand the foundational concepts needed to employ this weaponry most effectively.

You should begin by inviting Holy Spirit to assist in guiding you through the chapters. Make sure that you are in a quiet place with minimal distractions, bring your bible, and something to write with. Although you will be writing in your workbook, bring an extra note book just in case the revelations received take more writing space than the book allows. I also recommend that you bring a box of tissues. During this journey, Holy Spirit will undoubtedly bring up memories, situations, and circumstances that have been hidden deep inside so that you can identify root issues. Be prepared for a time of great revelation, discomfort, and healing as you make your way through the chapters designed to lead you down a path to wholeness.

As each chapter is read, go to the corresponding chapter in the workbook. Prayerfully, answer the questions . . . take your time. Allow Holy Spirit to speak to you and shine the light of truth from the Word of God into those dark places of the unknown within your soul. Don't be afraid to laugh, cry, sing, praise, etc. Allow yourself to be emptied out as you respond to Holy Spirit's loving prompts. It may some time to complete a chapter of the workbook, that's okay. During this time you are in the counseling room of heaven and God himself is performing a massive overhaul in your being. He is changing, removing, and re-arranging those parts of you that have been broken, wounded, and fragmented. Allow his love, compassion, and healing virtue to permeate those places. Submit to his working and partake of the fruit of generational deliverance that he is offering to you and your bloodline.

There are five appendices located in the back of this workbook that contain other resources that will enable the reader to succeeded in performing generational warfare. Appendix A provides step by step instruction on how to utilize the Generational Deliverance technique information as a prayer focus. It includes a sample template that has been completed using examples gathered from the **Breaking the Back of Generational Curses** text. Appendix B contain a sample template to be filled out by the individual. Appendix C contain a sample template for use in addressing generational bondages that affect those in leadership. Appendix D contain a Generational Deliverance Prayer template and Appendix E contain the scriptures outlining blessing and curses as recorded in Deuteronomy, chapter 28.

Part I: Assessment

Section 1: Identifying the Problem

In this section, I recount the circumstances that prompted me to begin my journey towards generational deliverance. I believe that you are here now because you too have identified some problem areas in yourself or your bloodline and are seeking the answer on how to address them. But remember, the journey towards generational deliverance for the family is foremost a journey towards personal deliverance, and God has promised to save YOU and YOUR households. (Acts 16:31)

It's easy to become overwhelmed by the problems we see as we look ourselves through our bloodline. In addition, the use of this tool will cause a magnification of those problems as you press forward in discovery. Therefore, it is important that we keep the promises that God has made to ourselves and our family in our eye-gate and rehearse them in our ear-gate so that we will not be overcome by feelings of regret, anger, sorrow, or despair. To this end, we will begin our journey by girding up our loins with the truth of God's Word concerning his faithfulness. (Ephesians 6:14a)

Again, it is paramount that one understand that this spiritual journey cannot be used properly without the expressed guidance of Holy Spirit. As you undergo the leadership of Holy Spirit review these scriptures, allow your faith to arise and begin to build a bridge that will escort you/family to the place of deliverance that you long to see.

The information attained while completing this workbook can provide a focal point for your intercession and is considered the backbone of the Generational Deliverance prayer strategy. When the sinful root in relationship to a curse is identified and the Generational Deliverance technique is applied, the resulting action will provide a transformation that can be monitored. In other words, once the root sin of the problem has been identified and the Generational Deliverance technique has been applied, there will be a decrease in the presence or strength of the demonic manifestation that can be actively tracked and documented. This decrease may be gradual or sudden depending on various factors such as the length of time the bondage has been intact, the sin committed that allowed the bondage, and the strength of anointing present to break the bondage.

- **Deuteronomy 7:9 –** *"Know therefore that the Lord your God, He is God, the faithful God, who keeps His covenant and His lovingkindness to a thousandth generation with those who love Him and keep His commandments."*

- **I Corinthians 10:13 –** *"No temptation has overtaken you but such as is common to man; and God is faithful, who will not allow you to be tempted beyond what you are able, but with the temptation will provide the way of escape also, so that you will be able to endure it."*

- **Lamentations 3:22-23 –** *"For the Lord's loving kindnesses indeed never cease, For His compassions never fail. They are new every morning; Great is Your faithfulness".*

- **Numbers 23:19 –** *"God is not a man, that He should lie, nor a son of man, that He should repent; Has He said, and will He not do it? Or has He spoken, and will He not make it good?"*

- **Joshua 21:45 –** *"Not one of the good promises which the Lord had made to the house of Israel failed; all came to pass".*

- **2 Corinthians 1:20 –** *"For as many as are the promises of God, in Him they are yes; therefore also through Him is our Amen to the glory of God through us"*

REFLECTION

A. Identify a sinful pattern of behavior that you have struggled with and list it here.

_____

_____

_____

B. Have you noted that sinful pattern in others in your family? If yes, who is it and what is their relationship to you in the family?

_____

_____

_____

C. How far back has this sinful pattern (iniquity) been identified within the family line?

_____

_____

_____

NOTE: *The longer a sinful pattern has been in a bloodline, the harder it can be to overcome. In some instances, you are not just struggling against the sinful pattern itself, but you are also struggling with the strength produced by all of the other members in your family who also participated in that sin. Family participation gives satan a legal right to rule the bloodline through that sin. With this insight in mind reflect on the previous answers you listed above. You can use this information to develop a prayer strategy. Use Appendix A as a guideline.*

Part II: Diagnosis

Section 1: Identifying the Solution

DEFINITIONS

Understanding the origin of a thing helps to understand its purpose. I believe this is especially true as you begin to understand the concept of generational deliverance.

1. Using the text define each generational deliverance concepts listed below.

   A. Sin _____

   B. Iniquity _____

   C. Curse _____

   D. Generation/Bloodline _____

   E. Demonic Attachment _____

   F. Generational Curse _____

NOTE: *According to the text, generational deliverance is defined as the process of breaking perverse traits or the Generational Deliverance technique an individual or bloodline through the removal of the demonic entity assigned to produce injury to it.*

Section 2: The Origin of Generational Curses

Review the origin of generational curses located in Genesis, Chapter 3 then answer the following questions.

1. How did Adam disobey God's command?

_____

_____

_____

_____

_____

_____

_____

2. Who did Eve blame for her decision to eat the fruit in the Garden of Eden?

_____

_____

_____

_____

_____

_____

_____

3. In Genesis, Chapter 3 there are three incidences of the first family trying to hide from God. List them here.

_____

_____

_____

_____

_____

_____

_____

4. According to the text what was the iniquitous pattern identified in the first family?

_____

_____

_____

_____

_____

_____

_____

Section 3: God as Judge

1. Name three attributes (names) for Jehovah/God and what they signify.

A. _____

B. _____

C. _____

2. What does Psalm 89:4 say about God as Judge; and why is this an important truth for those who perform generational deliverance to know?

_____

_____

_____

_____

_____

_____

3. According to the text how did God reveal himself as a righteous Judge in the case of the disobedience of Adam and Eve?

_____

_____

_____

_____

_____

_____

4. List the judgment released against Adam, Eve and the Serpent.

_____

_____

_____

_____

_____

5. Do you think the judgment released against them was fair, why or why not?

_____

_____

_____

_____

_____

_____

6. Exodus 34:6-7 is a foundational scripture for the concept of generational deliverance. Express this scripture's meaning in your own words.

_____

_____

_____

_____

_____

7. Every judge has a courtroom. Where is God's courtroom? Describe what it looks like below. See Hebrews 12:22-23 and Daniel 7:9-10.

_____

_____

_____

_____

_____

_____

8. Who can enter the courtroom of God?

_____

_____

_____

_____

_____

_____

REFLECTION

A. Do you know anyone who has ever participated in a court proceeding. Did the individual represent the prosecutor or defendant? Was justice served?

_____

_____

_____

B. Do you think God is just, fair, or both? Why?

_____

_____

_____

C. Give an example of a situation in which you felt unjustly treated? What was your response?

_____

_____

_____

NOTE: *I believe that fair is a word used to express the concept of equality and is based on the human standard of morality which can change. However, God's standard of justice will always overrule man's sense of fairness and is rendered based on his Holiness which never changes no matter who is involved and what is done.*

Section 4: Sin's Penalty

1. Describe the Tabernacle of Moses. (See Exodus 25:10-40, 26,27).

_____

_____

_____

_____

_____

_____

_____

2. This is an important concept for Generational Deliverance. Why do you think this is so?

_____

_____

_____

_____

_____

_____

_____

_____

3. State Leviticus 17:11 in your own words. In light of this truth what is the ONLY PAYMENT/ATONEMENT THAT CAN BE USED FOR SIN? (Hebrews 9:22)

_____

_____

_____

_____

_____

4. Why is this information relevant to the concept of generational deliverance?

_____

_____

_____

_____

_____

_____

_____

5. Define the word repent.

_____

_____

_____

_____

_____

_____

_____

6. According to the text, what is a *Blood Account*™ and who has one?

_____

_____

_____

_____

_____

_____

_____

_____

7. Romans 8:2 states that, *"The Law of the Spirit of Life in Christ Jesus has set me free from the Law of Sin and Death."* What does this mean in relation to the concept of generational deliverance?

_____

_____

_____

_____

_____

_____

_____

_____

8. Identify the only individual capable of paying the price for sin and iniquity. Why is this so?

_____

_____

_____

_____

_____

_____

_____

_____

_____

REFLECTION

A. Do you recall a time as a child when you did something that resulted in your receiving severe punishment? What was it?

_____

_____

_____

_____

_____

B. Did you know that you were wrong, why or why not?

_____

_____

_____

_____

_____

C. Now, how you do think you would have felt if the authority figure suddenly decided to remove the punishment? Why?

_____

_____

_____

_____

_____

NOTE: *Generational Deliverance is the removal of curses through the atoning sacrifice of the blood of Jesus.*

Section 5:
How Does Generational Deliverance Work?

1. One example used in the text to explain how the Generational Deliverance technique works is the Hemp plant. According to the text, what is the significance of using this plant?

_____

_____

_____

_____

_____

2. Another example used in the text is a large tree with many branches. Why is this analogy significant?

_____

_____

_____

_____

_____

3. Can you think of another analogy that can explain how this spiritual tool works?

_____

_____

_____

_____

_____

4. According to the text, how does a demonic spirit attach to an individual in a bloodline?

_____

_____

_____

_____

_____

_____

5. Define the three major elements that define a human being according to I Thessalonians 5:3.

Spirit _____

_____

_____

Soul _____

_____

_____

Body _____

_____

_____

6. According to the text, name the four compartments of the soul and their functions.

_____

_____

_____

_____

_____

7. According to the text what two scriptures identify the need for soul restoration or healing?

_____

_____

_____

_____

_____

NOTE: *The elements of the soul assist in determining the type of personality an individual will develop. They are affected both negatively and positively by normal and abnormal situations that make up the human experience. Injuries to the soul are inflicted through various circumstances throughout an individual's life such as trauma from an accident, or pain from a divorce.*

8. According to the text what happens to the soul of an individual who continues to commits sin or iniquitous acts?

_____

_____

_____

_____

_____

_____

_____

_____

9. According to the text what does the symptoms of a soul injured by sin produce?

_____

_____

_____

_____

_____

_____

_____

_____

REFLECTION

A. List some traumatic experiences that you have encountered that may have left your soul injured?

_____

_____

_____

_____

_____

_____

B. What are some of the ways that you can tell your soul has been injured?

_____

_____

_____

_____

_____

_____

NOTE: *According to the text "a generational curse is the result of God's judgment on a repetitious sinful act perpetrated by a family line. It gives a demonic entity the legal right to attach itself to individuals or a family line for the expressed purpose of causing injury."*

Section 6: Generational Deliverance, Why Now?

1. According to the text, generational deliverance is released in this season by God to assist the body of Christ to enter into her _____

2. List the five restorative movements, their dates, and the spiritual truths released.

A. _____

_____

_____

B. _____

_____

_____

C. _____

_____

_____

D. _____

_____

_____

E. _____

_____

_____

3. List the five-fold ministry gifts. Why were they given to the church?

_____

_____

_____

_____

_____

_____

4. Define the "Kingdom Movement" and explain its focus according to Matthew 28:19.

_____

_____

_____

_____

_____

_____

5. Explain how Matthew 3:10 and the "Kingdom Movement" affect the need for the Generational Deliverance technique within the Body of Christ in this season.

_____

_____

_____

_____

_____

_____

Section 7: The Purpose and Characteristics of Curses

1. According to the text, these two scriptures listed below explain why satan utilizes curses. Why is this information significant?

Genesis 6:1-2 _____

_____

_____

_____

_____

_____

_____

_____

Numbers 22:3-6 _____

_____

_____

_____

_____

_____

_____

_____

_____

2. What is the ultimate goal of a curse? (Deuteronomy 28:45)

_____

_____

_____

_____

_____

3. According to the text, what is one way a "born again believer" can tell if a curse is working against themselves or a family member in bondage?

_____

_____

_____

_____

_____

NOTE: *We learned within the text that a generational curse is a judgment against unrepentant sin or iniquity on a generation or bloodline. But what does a curse look like? Deuteronomy 28:15-45 provides the biblical view on how generational curses look when in operation. Review the Appendix E again for this scripture reading.*

4. Curses are revealed in various ways, however, according to the text there is one characteristic of curses that help identify them no matter where they're hidden. What is that characteristic?

_____

_____

_____

_____

5. Deuteronomy 28:20 reveal another characteristic of curses, what is it?

_____

_____

_____

_____

6. According to Deuteronomy 28:45 how long does a curse work?

_____

_____

_____

_____

7. The text presents an Old Testament example of an iniquitous pattern first noted in Genesis 12:13 and identified again in Genesis 26:7. Identify the iniquitous pattern. Who was it revealed in?

_____

_____

_____

_____

REFLECTION-PART I

Do you have any family members that function in a leadership role? Make a list of them. Identify any pattern of character weaknesses or sinful practices. Make a list and place the information next to the appropriate family member. You can use the chart located in Appendix C in the back of this workbook. Once you have completed this portion of the chart continue to the next section.

_____

_____

_____

_____

_____

_____

_____

_____

_____

_____

_____

_____

_____

_____

_____

_____

_____

_____

Part III: Implementation

Section 1: Implementing the Solution

Use the text to fill in the blanks:

1. According to the text, _____ is the foundational concept of generational deliverance. What is the purpose of intercession?

    This prayer format utilized for Generational Deliverance is first modeled in the Old Testament through the Levitical Priesthood. However, in the New Testament, Jesus Christ has become our example as he is our high priest and chief intercessor (Hebrews 4:14-16, 7:25)

2. Another definition of intercessor is "one who _____ for another."

3. According to the text, the process of generational deliverance begins with _____ by the intercessor for the _____ or _____ behavior performed by _____ or their _____.

4. Next, the Blood of Jesus must be applied by the _____ to the Mercy Seat of God on behalf of the sin or iniquitous acts of their family so that forgiveness of the trespass can be released.

5. Once the _____ has been applied to the Mercy Seat the _____ of forgiveness can be attained for the intercessor or their family member.

6. The text explains that it is _____ that takes away satan's _____ right to perpetuate _____ generational curses.

7. Once satan's legal right to perpetuate the curse is broken, God the father can be petitioned to release _____, and _____ in the name of Jesus to the individual or family members.

8. State the *Law of Spiritual Authority.*™

_____

_____

_____

_____

_____

9. The *Law of Spiritual Authority*™ is an important law to understand when performing the Generational Deliverance technique, why is this?

_____

_____

_____

_____

_____

10. Matthew 28:19-20 and Acts 1:8 are scriptures that provide assurance to the believer that they have been fully equipped to handle satan and his tactics. How does this truth affect one's ability to perform the Generational Deliverance technique?

_____

_____

_____

_____

_____

REFLECTION-PART II

Now review the information that you placed in Appendix C, on page 33. Identify any duplication of sinful behavior patterns among the family members listed. These behavior patterns may suggest that a specific satanic assignment has been launched against the bloodline to hinder the family's generational assignment within the earth. See if you can detect the generational root-sin behind this family pattern. Be aware that the same sin can be revealed in different ways though different individuals. Use this information to assist you in developing a prayer focus through which you can implement the Generational Deliverance technique.

_____

_____

_____

_____

_____

_____

_____

_____

_____

_____

_____

_____

_____

_____

_____

_____

Section 2: Performing the Generational Deliverance Technique

Use the text to fill in the blanks:

1. Identify _____

2. Acknowledge to God _____
Ask Holy Spirit to bring to your remembrance _____

3. Repent _____
You must repent for yourself _____
This must be done _____

4. Apply _____ and decree _____
Do this until Holy Spirit releases you.

5. Release _____
Injuries to the soul _____
_____

6. Now you are ready _____
The sin has been cleansed and you have released healing on any injured area of the soul due to its performance.
Now _____
You may need to repeat this process more than once results you want to see.
_____, therefore results may be gradual. In addition,
everything in the Kingdom functions _____
Be patient, be persistent, and persevere.

NOTE: *If you follow the above steps and nothing happens that means that something else is happening. The enemy still has the legal right to stay. You must ask Holy Spirit to show you where Satan has retained legal right in this situation.*

REFLECTION

A. What are three spiritual disciplines that every believers must do in order to promote spiritual growth?

_____

_____

_____

_____

_____

_____

B. What is the one foundational spiritual discipline that every believer needs to be consistent in order to perform Generational Deliverance?

_____

_____

_____

_____

_____

_____

C. Although the discipline of prayer promotes spiritual growth, it also produces something even more important and that is?

_____

_____

_____

_____

_____

_____

Part IV: Evaluation

Section 1: Evaluating the Solution

In this section, the three guidelines used to determine the use of Generational Deliverance are reviewed. These guidelines are in alignment with the revelation presented concerning the need for discernment when assessing for generational curses given by Jesus in John, Chapter 9. Use the text to fill in the blanks:

1. First _____
Use of the Generational Deliverance technique is a spiritual weapon that must be

_____

2. Second, _____

_____

_____

generational bondages are usually _____ and removing the layers takes time.

3. Third, _____

_____

The Generational Deliverance technique may need to be utilized with other conventional spiritual warfare weapons such as fasting, and counseling in order to achieve maximum results.

Appendix A

Developing a Prayer Focus Using the Generational Deliverance Technique

STEP #1

Identify the sin, weakness, problem, trauma - Place in Column A

STEP#2

Identify the generational component - how is the curse revealed in you or your bloodline. Place answer in column B. If the problem does not have generational component, the Generational Deliverance Technique may be not required to address the issue. A review of your family history and communicating with Holy Spirit concerning the problem is key to accurately performing this step.

STEP #3

Identify the generational or root sin. Place this information in column C. - Ask Holy Spirit to reveal the sin committed by yourself/bloodline through review of The Word of God - Start with Duet 28 chapter. Speaking with family members can also provide the revelation needed to assist in you in identifying the generational root of sinful practices performed by your bloodline.

STEP #4

Once you identify the root or generational sin, you can plug information into the generational deliverance template Repentance Prayer formula listed in Appendix C

STEP #5

Identify how the curse has been broken. Document your results. Place this information in Column D

Below is a sample of how to use the generational deliverance prayer strategy to develop a prayer focus using the example scenarios presented in the Evaluation section of the BBGC text.

Name	COLUMN A Curse/Problem Trauma	COLUMN B Family Manifestation	COLUMN C Generational Root Sin	COLUMN D Evaluation of Generational Deliverance
Nita	Unforgiveness	Hold grudges	Show No Mercy	Ability to forgive coworker
Cynthia	Spoken against by children	Children speak against mother to others	Father tried to Injure mother	Children apologized Confirmed allegiance to mother
Nita	Fear	Inconsistent faith	Premeditated Violence toward others	Supernatural increase in faith
Dorothy	Kidney Failure	Family death from Cancer	Sin of the Father	Delivered from Kidney Failure
Mom	Blood clots in legs	Previous family death from blood clot in leg	Sin of the Father	Acceleration of healing of blood clot

NOTE: *The information provided within this chart can be utilized in providing a focal point for prayer and is considered the backbone of the Generational Deliverance prayer strategy. When the sinful root in relationship to a curse is identified and GD is applied, the resulting action will provide situational data that can be monitored. In other words, once the root sin of the problem has been identified and the generational deliverance technique has been applied there will be a decrease in the presence or strength of the demonic manifestation that can be actively tracked and documented. This decrease may be gradual or sudden depending on various factors such as the length of time the bondage has been intact, the sin committed that allowed the bondage, the strength of anointing present to break the bondage.*

Appendix B

Generational Deliverance
Prayer Strategy Guideline

Name	COLUMN A	COLUMN B	COLUMN C	COLUMN D
	Curse/Problem Trauma	Family Manifestation	Generational Root Sin	Evaluation of Generational Deliverance

Appendix C

Generational Deliverance Prayer
Focus for Family Leaders

Name	Family Member	Leadership Role	Problem/Weakness	Generational Sin

Appendix D

Generational Deliverance Prayer

Father God in the name of Jesus, I thank you for the promise of salvation given to me through your son Jesus Christ. I thank you that you are Adonai, my Lord and Master, and Elohim, my creator. I thank you that you are my king, judge, lawgiver, and you will save both me from any and all attacks of the enemy. (Isaiah 33:22) I thank you that you have sent your son Jesus to earth to represent your love for mankind. I declare that Jesus is my Lord, Savior, Mediator, and Substitute for sin. Thank you, Jesus for shedding your precious blood, so that I now have a right to the Tree of Life. I thank you Jesus that because of your shed blood I can receive the inheritance of the blessings of Abraham for me and my bloodline. I ask that you would manifest your Kingdom on earth as it is in Heaven.

I thank you that I am your child and you are my God. I say that I have been translated out of the Kingdom of Darkness and placed into the Kingdom of your dear Son. I thank you that part of my inheritance as a son in the Kingdom of God is the ability to have my sins taken away by the blood of Jesus. Your word says that if I confess my sins. Jesus is faithful and just to forgive me of my sin and cleanse me from all unrighteousness. (I John 1:9) I now confess the sin/sins of _____ for me and my bloodline. I confess that this sin/sins is/are against your Word and so it/they are wrong. I take full responsibility for the act of sin and ask that you would cleanse me/family/bloodline from all unrighteousness or uncleanness. I apply the blood of Jesus to the mercy seat in heaven and so receive the atonement for that sin. Jesus I now ask that you would heal any injuries to my soul present due to my participation in the sin/sins committed. I release the resurrection power of God to heal every injured place and bring to life any area in me that experienced death as result of committing this sin.

Now Satan I bind your every work against me/family in the area of _____. I cancel every satanic assignment that has been released as a result of committing this sin. I say the enemy can no longer keep me/ family from my/our kingdom assignment through participation in this sin. I decree that the path of the righteous shines bright as the noonday sun (Proverbs 4:18) giving me/us wisdom and clarity concerning the strategies that satan has used to cause me/ us to sabotage my/our own kingdom destiny. I reverse every curse that has been released on me as a result of this sin and deem it null and void. I lose the plan and assignment of God for myself /family and declare that I/we receive the assignment and fully submit to the call of God for my life/family. I pull down the satanic government that has ruled over my head and over the head of my bloodline through the participation of this/these sins, and replace it with the government of God through our Lord and Savior Jesus Christ. I say that Jesus is Lord over me and my family and we are citizens of heaven who are governed by the Spirit of Life in Christ Jesus instead of the law of sin and death. We release this prayer in Jesus name Amen, and so be it.

Appendix E

Deuteronomy 28:1-68 (NASB)

"Now, if you diligently obey the voice of the LORD, your God, carefully observing all his commandments which I give you today, the LORD, your God, will set you high above all the nations of the earth. 2 All these blessings will come upon you and overwhelm you when you obey the voice of the LORD, your God: 3 May you be blessed in the city, and blessed in the country!"

4 "Blessed be the fruit of your womb, the produce of your soil and the offspring of your livestock, the issue of your herds and the young of your flocks!"

5 "Blessed be your grain basket and your kneading bowl!"

6 "May you be blessed in your coming in, and blessed in your going out Victory and Prosperity. 7 The LORD will beat down before you the enemies that rise up against you; they will come out against you from one direction, and flee before you in seven. 8 The LORD will affirm the blessing upon you, on your barns and on all your undertakings; he will bless you in the land that the LORD, your God, is giving you. 9 The LORD will establish you as a holy people, as he swore to you, if you keep the commandments of the LORD, your God, and walk in his ways. 10 All the peoples of the earth will see that the name of the LORD is proclaimed over you,* and they will be afraid of you. 11 The LORD will generously increase the fruit of your womb, the offspring of your livestock, and the produce of your soil, upon the land which the LORD swore to your ancestors he would give you. 12 The LORD will open up for you his rich storehouse, the heavens, to give your land rain in due season and to bless all the works of your hands. You will lend to many nations but borrow from none."

13 "The LORD will make you the head not the tail, the top not the bottom, if you obey the commandments of the LORD, your God, which I am giving you today, observing them carefully, 14 not turning aside, either to the right or to the left, from any of the words which I am giving you today, following other gods and serving them."

CURSES FOR DISOBEDIENCE.

15 "But if you do not obey the voice of the LORD, your God, carefully observing all his commandments and statutes which I give you today, all these curses shall come upon you and overwhelm you:"

16 "May you be cursed in the city, and cursed in the country! 17 Cursed be your grain basket and your kneading bowl! 18 Cursed be the fruit of your womb, the produce of your soil and the offspring of your livestock, the issue of your herds and the young of your flocks! 19 May you be cursed in your coming in, and cursed in your going out!

SICKNESS AND DEFEAT.

20 "The LORD will send on you a curse, panic, and frustration in everything you set your hand to, until you are speedily destroyed and perish for the evil you have done in forsaking me. 21 The LORD will make disease cling to you until he has made an end of you from the land you are entering to possess."

22 "The LORD will strike you with consumption, fever, and inflammation, with fiery heat and drought, with blight and mildew that will pursue you until you perish. 23 The heavens over your heads will be like bronze and the earth under your feet like iron. 24 For rain the LORD will give your land powdery dust, which will come down upon you from the heavens until you are destroyed. 25 The LORD will let you be beaten down before your enemies; though you advance against them from one direction, you will flee before them in seven, so that you will become an object of horror to all the kingdoms of the earth. 26 Your corpses will become food for all the birds of the air and for the beasts of the field, with no one to frighten them off."

27 "The LORD will strike you with Egyptian boils and with tumors, skin diseases and the itch, from none of which you can be cured. 28 And the LORD will strike you with

madness, blindness and panic, 29 so that even at midday you will grope in the dark as though blind, unable to find your way. Despoilment. You will be oppressed and robbed continually, with no one to come to your aid. 30 Though you betroth a wife, another will have her. Though you build a house, you will not live in it. Though you plant a vineyard, you will not pluck its fruits."

31 "Your ox will be slaughtered before your eyes, but you will not eat its flesh. Your donkey will be stolen in your presence, but you will never get it back. Your flocks will be given to your enemies, with no one to come to your aid. 32 Your sons and daughters will be given to another people while you strain your eyes looking for them every day, having no power to do anything. 33 A people you do not know will consume the fruit of your soil and of all your labor, and you will be thoroughly oppressed and continually crushed, 34 until you are driven mad by what your eyes must look upon."

35 "The LORD will strike you with malignant boils of which you cannot be cured, on your knees and legs, and from the soles of your feet to the crown of your head."

EXILE.

36 "The LORD will bring you, and your king whom you have set over you, to a nation which you and your ancestors have not known, and there you will serve other gods, of wood and stone, 37 and you will be a horror, a byword, a taunt among all the peoples to which the LORD will drive you."

FRUITLESS LABORS.

38 "Though you take out seed to your field, you will harvest but little, for the locusts will devour it. 39 Though you plant and cultivate vineyards, you will not drink or store up the wine, for the worms will eat them. 40 Though you have olive trees throughout your country, you will have no oil for ointment, for your olives will drop off. 41 Though you beget sons and daughters, they will not remain with you, for they will go into captivity. 42 Buzzing insects will take possession of all your trees and the crops of your soil. 43 The resident aliens among you will rise above you higher and higher, while you sink lower and lower. 44 They will lend to you, not you to them. They will become the head, you the tail."

45 All these curses will come upon you, pursuing you and overwhelming you, until you are destroyed, because you would not obey the voice of the LORD, your God, by keeping his commandments and statutes which he gave you. 46 They will be a sign and a wonder or you and your descendants for all time."

47 "Since you would not serve the LORD, your God, with heartfelt joy for abundance of every kind, 48 in hunger and thirst, in nakedness and utter want, you will serve the enemies whom the LORD will send against you. He will put an iron yoke on your neck, until he destroys you."

INVASION AND SIEGE.

49 The LORD will raise up against you a nation from afar, from the end of the earth, that swoops down like an eagle, a nation whose language you do not understand, 50 nation of fierce appearance that shows neither respect for the aged nor mercy for the young. 51 They will consume the offspring of your livestock and the produce of your soil, until you are destroyed; they will leave you no grain or wine or oil, no issue of herd, no young of flock, until they have brought about your ruin. 52 They will besiege you in each of your communities, until the great, fortified walls, in which you trust, come tumbling down all over your land. They will besiege you in every community throughout the land which the LORD, your God, has given you, 53 and because of the siege and the distress to which your enemy subjects you, you will eat the fruit of your womb, the flesh of your own sons and daughters whom the LORD, your God, has given you."

54 "The most refined and fastidious man among you will begrudge his brother and his beloved wife and his surviving children, 55 any share in the flesh of his children that he himself is using for food because nothing else is left him—such the siege and distress to which your enemy will subject you in all your communities. 56 The most fastidious woman among you, who would not venture to set the sole of her foot on the ground, so refined and fastidious is she, will begrudge her beloved husband and her son and daughter 57 the afterbirth that issues from her womb and the infants she brings forth because she secretly eats them for want of anything else—such the siege and distress to which your enemy will subject you in your communities."

PLAGUES.

58 "If you are not careful to observe all the words of this law which is written in this book, and to fear this glorious and awesome name, the LORD, your God, 59 the LORD will bring upon you and your descendants wondrous calamities, severe and constant calamities, and malignant and constant sicknesses. 60 He will bring back upon you all the diseases of Egypt* which you dread, and they will cling to you. 61 Even any sickness or calamity not written in this book of the law, that too the LORD will bring upon you until you are destroyed. 62 You who were numerous as the stars of the heavens will be left few in number, because you would not obey the voice of the LORD, your God."

EXILE.

63 "Just as the LORD once took delight in making you prosper and grow, so will the LORD now take delight in ruining and destroying you, and you will be plucked out of the land you are now entering to possess. 64 The LORD will scatter you among all the peoples from one end of the earth to the other, and there you will serve other gods, of wood and stone, which you and your ancestors have not known. 65 Among these nations you will find no rest, not even a resting place for the sole of your foot, for there the LORD will give you an anguished heart and wearied eyes and a trembling spirit. 66 Your life will hang in suspense and you will stand in dread both day and night, never sure of your life."

67 "In the morning you will say, "Would that it were evening!" and in the evening you will say, "Would that it were morning!" because of the dread that your heart must feel and the sight that your eyes must see. 68 The LORD will send you back in ships to Egypt, by a route which I told you that you would never see again; and there you will offer yourselves for sale to your enemies as male and female slaves, but there will be no buyer."

About the Author

Doneita Harmon was born in Chicago, Illinois and is the 3rd of 6 children. She received her high school education at Proviso East High school in Maywood, Illinois during which time she accepted Christ as her personal Lord and Savior. In her senior year of high school, the family moved to Mississippi, where her college career began. She later met and married her husband Lenard Harmon a member of the Armed Forces. For the next 20 years, Doneita traveled the world as a military spouse walking in the call to build up her household as a godly wife and mother.

After 20 years, Doneita resumed her educational pursuits and has not stopped. She successfully obtained a Bachelor's Degree in Nursing and a Master's Degree in Nursing Education. During that time Doneita received membership to the Sigma Theta Tau Nursing Honor Society. She has provided a strong voice advocating for nurses within the Public Health arena and appeared before both county and state legislatures as well as The Board of Registered Nursing in California. She has also served in various positions within the church including praise team leader, Sunday school teacher, and assistant mission's director. Doneita is currently a licensed, ordained minister and lead instructor at Living Praise Christian Center.

Doneita has done in-depth research and study about generational curses and has authored her first book, Breaking the Back of Generation Curses: A Journey to Wholeness. The workbook will be coming soon, and she created a line of products to be released, that will assist individuals in identifying and addressing generational issues. The generational deliverance product line includes books, workbooks, devotionals, and a genogram to help families in identifying generational patterns. She is also working on a second Master's Degree in Marriage and Family Counseling. Doneita is an inventor, intercessory prayer warrior, songwriter, and keynote speaker.

Doneita and her husband have been married for more than 33 years, and they have three adult children, two sons, and one daughter.

If you would like to receive more information about generational curses please see my second book, Hidden Covenants and Demonic Judgments. This book explains the importance of covenant in the life of a believer and how Christians and their families are paying satanic debts of which they are not aware.

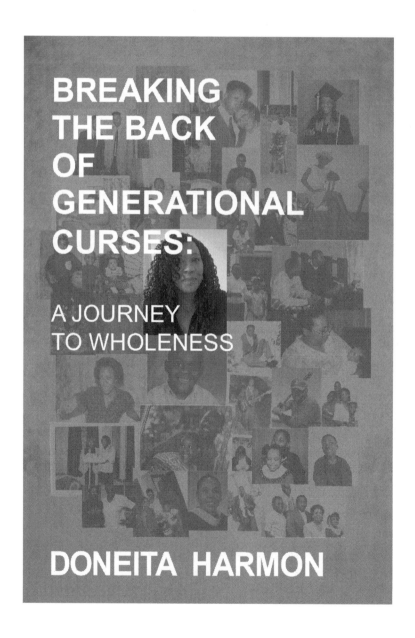

Made in the USA
Middletown, DE
27 April 2022

64818073R00040